INDIE AUTHOR MAGAZINE

HELLO AND WELCOME!

I'm Indie Annie, and I'm thrilled you're reading this gorgeous full-color version of IAM. Did you know that you can also access all the information, education, and inspiration in our app? It's available on both the iOS App Store and Google Play. And for those that prefer to listen to me read articles, you can pop over to Spotify or our website. Happy Reading!

X

IndieAuthorMagazine.com

Download on the
App Store

GET IT ON
Google Play

Spotify

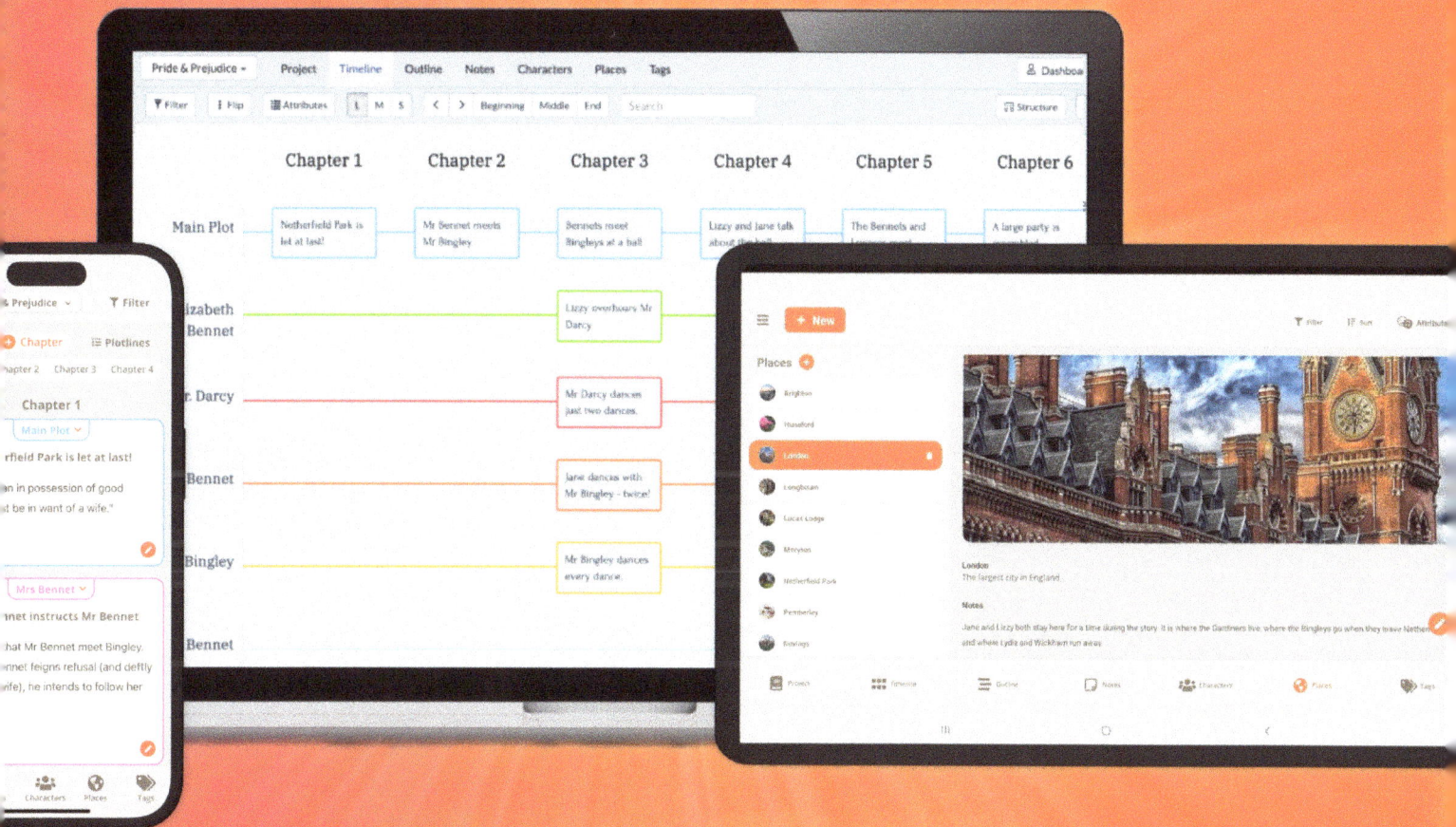

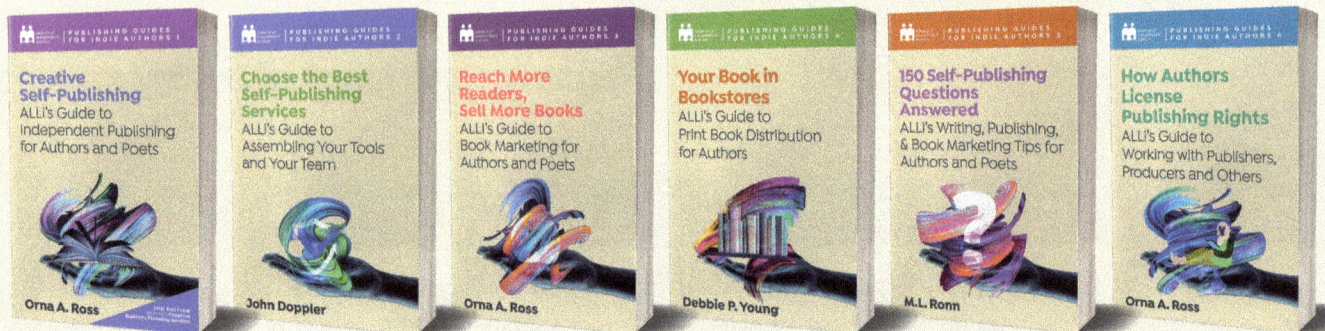

I joined while having a crisis with Amazon KDP... The Alliance is a beacon of light. I recommend that all indie authors join...

Susan Marshall

The Alliance is about standing together.

Joanna Penn

It's the good stuff, all on one place.

Richard Wright

"ALLi has helped me in myriad ways: discounts on services, vetting providers, charting a course to sales success. But more than anything it's a community of friendly, knowledgeable, helpful people."

Beth Duke

See hundreds more testimonials at:
AllianceIndependentAuthors.org/testimonials

IAM

THE BUSINESS OF WRITING

Authorpreneurs in Action

"I love Lulu! They've been a fantastic distributor of my paperbacks and an excellent partner as I dive into direct sales. They integrate so smoothly with my personal Shopify store, and their customer support has been top notch."

Katie Cross, katiecrossbooks.com

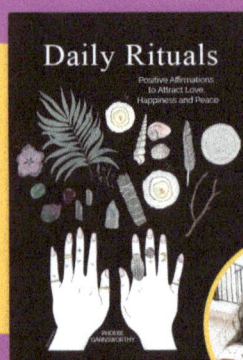

"Having my own store has given me the freedom to look at my creativity as a profitable business and lifelong career."

Phoebe Garnsworthy, phoebegarnsworthy.com

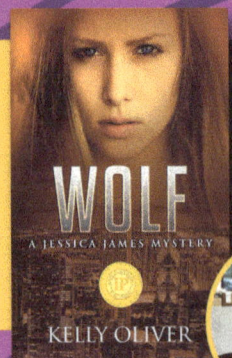

"Lulu has a super handy integration with Shopify. Lulu makes it so easy to sell paperbacks directly to readers."

Kelly Oliver, kellyoliverbooks.com

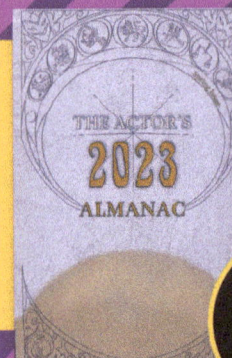

"My experience with Lulu Direct has been more convenient and simple than I anticipated or thought possible. I simply publish, take a step back and allow the well-oiled machine to run itself. Most grateful!"

Molly McGivern, theactorsalmanac.com

INDIE
AUTHOR MAGAZINE

EDITORIAL

Publisher | Chelle Honiker

Editor in Chief | Nicole Schroeder

Creative Director | Alice Briggs

ADVERTISING & MARKETING

Inquiries
Ads@AtheniaCreative.com

Information
https://IndieAuthorMagazine.com/
advertising/

CONTRIBUTORS

Angela Archer, Elaine Bateman, Maureen Bonatch, Patricia Carr, Bradley Charbonneau, Honorée Corder, Jackie Dana, Heather Clement Davis, Jamie Davis, Laurel Decher, Fatima Fayez, Gill Fernley, Greg Fishbone, Jen B. Green, Jac Harmon, Marion Hermannsen, Steve Higgs, Chrishaun Keller-Hanna, Kasia Lasinska, Monica Leonelle, Jenn Lessmann, Megan Linski-Fox, Craig Martelle, Angie Martin, Merri Maywether Kevin McLaughlin, Lasairiona McMaster, Jenn Mitchell, Tanya Nellestein, Russell Nohelty, Susan Odev, Eryka Parker, Tiffany Robinson, Clare Sager, Joe Solari, Becca Syme, David Viergutz

SUBSCRIPTIONS
https://indieauthormagazine.com/subscribe/

HOW TO READ
https://indieauthormagazine.com/how-to-read/

WHEN WRITING MEANS BUSINESS
IndieAuthorMagazine.com

Athenia Creative | 6820 Apus Dr., Sparks, NV, 89436 USA | 775.298.1925
ISSN 2768-7880 (online)–ISSN 2768-7872 (print)

Another year is nearly complete, and I feel confident saying it's been a busy one for most of us. It's one of the side effects of being an indie author, after all. Generally, the word "leisurely" is not in our vocabulary.

If you're anything like me, at this point, your schedule is probably filled with last-minute to-dos as you prepare for the holidays—another chapter to write, a final invoice to pay, a few more social media posts to schedule. Or maybe you've planned ahead and are taking this month as a reset button. Instead of looking at what you want to finish in 2023, these last couple of weeks of the year will be about setting goals for the next one.

I won't pretend I'm not jealous of people in the second group; I've always wished I could be the person who "cleaned house" before a vacation, so to speak. But no matter which group you're in, it's important to recognize both approaches are valid. The same advice we've heard about writing—that no one can tell the story you've imagined except you—can apply to our businesses as well. And as we'll explore in this month's issue, there's no right way to manage any part of your career. We're all carving our own paths in this industry, whether that's in the stories we write, the financial decisions we make, or the tools we use. Take a moment to celebrate what you've already accomplished, then keep creating the stories your readers want in the way that works best for you.

On that note, thank you for trusting *Indie Author Magazine* to help you find your path this year. We hope you have a safe and happy holiday season, and we look forward to sharing more industry insights with you in 2024!

Nicole Schroeder
Editor in Chief
Indie Author Magazine

Nicole Schroeder is a storyteller at heart. As the editor in chief of Indie Author Magazine, she brings nearly a decade of journalism and editorial experience to the publication, delighting in any opportunity to tell true stories and help others do the same. She holds a bachelor's degree from the Missouri School of Journalism and minors in English and Spanish. Her previous work includes editorial roles at local publications, and she's helped edit and produce numerous fiction and nonfiction books, including a Holocaust survivor's memoir, alongside independent publishers. Her own creative writing has been published in national literary magazines. When she's not at her writing desk, Nicole is usually in the saddle, cuddling her guinea pigs, or spending time with family. She loves any excuse to talk about Marvel movies and considers National Novel Writing Month its own holiday.

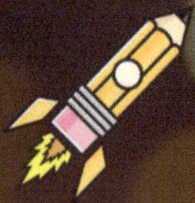

THE FUTURE OF PUBLISHING

A forward thinking,
exclusive conference
experience for authors
and small press publishers.

GET READY TO LOOK INTO THE FUTURE
HILTON RIVERSIDE NEW ORLEANS
FEBRUARY 26-29TH, 2024

futureofpublishingmastermind.com

ALLI EXCLUSIVE

Building a Business Mindset

For successful authors, writing is not just an art. It is also a business. In fact, the Alliance of Independent Authors (ALLi) refers to its top tier members, who have access to special benefits, such as a literary agent, as "authorpreneurs" because they are authors but also entrepreneurs. It's a mindset all authors who wish to be successful should consider adopting. And at each stage of your business, there are ways to develop that business mindset.

BEGINNERS

When starting out, some authors want to publish and not spend any money doing so. We know meeting professional publishing standards can create a financial barrier for some authors. A good cover, for example, can cost $500. A good editor can cost $700 to $1,200, depending on the length of your book. As part of its commitment to advocacy, ALLi offers a guide on how to self-publish for free, as we do not want finances to be a barrier to any writer. You can find the guide here: http://allianceindependentauthors.org/campaigns/selfpub3.

However, this can also point to a mindset shift that needs to happen when you decide to self-publish.

Self-published authors are publishers as well as writers, and publishing is a business. A business owner invests money to make more money, so you'll do best if you think more about return on investment than costs when it comes to certain expenses. This mindset shift can take time—and seeing some profits—before it sinks in, so start small. Instead of asking, "How much does it cost?" get into the habit of asking, "How much return can I expect on this investment once I can afford it?" There is no business where you would expect success without putting in at least a little money up front.

Another important part of building a business is having the right people around you. The term "self-publishing" implies you'll be doing everything on your own. In actuality, taking on every responsibility yourself will not only wear you out but also result in a lower quality product. Successful indie authors take the time to choose great cover designers, excellent editors, and professional software, among other elements, to lighten the load on themselves. ALLi's book *Choose the Best Self-Publishing Services: ALLi's Guide to Assembling Your Tools and Your Team* by John Doppler can be useful for choosing services that work for you, and ALLi's Vetted Services Directory has a comprehensive list of publishing services, all of whom have been checked for quality and value. Both are free to members and available for sale to non-members.

Self-published authors also benefit from collaborating with their fellow authors and being ready to learn new skills as they go along. Indie authors today are in a great position to learn from some of the most successful self-publishers. There is a wealth of excellent advice, both free and paid, within the industry, so even if you are new to self-publishing, you can confidently make good publishing plans and set them in motion. ALLi's book *Creative Self-Publishing* covers the seven processes of self-publishing, step by step. This is free for members or can be bought at ALLi's online bookstore, https://selfpublishingadvice.org/bookshop, by non-members. Chapters 20–23 cover distribution, marketing, promotion, and licensing rights.

EMERGING AUTHORS

As authors move on from those early days of publishing, their business mindset also grows. Parts 7 and 8 of *Creative Self-Publishing* focus on what it means to be a creative business and offer different business models to consider. Where many authors might begin with an exclusive model in which they only publish to Amazon, for example, others may consider other options, from "going wide," or publishing non-exclusively, to a "creator" model, which sees authors selling directly to readers and includes various products and services alongside books, such as premium digital content, subscriptions, memberships, reader clubs, paid video and audio content, crowdfunding, and/or patronage.

Many emerging authors may hope one day to pass on marketing work to an outside agency, but recent data has shown that the most successful indie authors still do their own marketing, even if they use tools or assistants to help, as they know their books and care about them more than anyone else. Some even enjoy putting on different "hats"— being a writer for part of their day and a marketer for the rest.

Marketing is a creative area of business work, so being a creative person already will stand you in good stead. Get to know your readers, then think about how to connect with them in new and engaging ways. ALLi has regular blog posts and podcast episodes on all aspects of marketing to give you new ideas on how to enliven your reader connections.

As your author career grows, be sure to set aside time for business just like you do for writing. Start by reading ALLi's Big Indie Author Data Drop report (https://allianceindependentauthors.org/facts), which is a visual guide to facts and figures about the self-publishing industry that all authors should know.

EXPERIENCED AUTHORS

Even the most experienced indie author can miss some business opportunities. It's worth taking strategic planning time away from your already successful writing and publishing business to consider what next steps you could take.

Seventy-five percent of indie authors have not put in place a will that covers their literary estate. In the US, books remain in copyright and can make money for seventy years after the author's death, if well managed, so this can be a big missed opportunity. Setting up such a will and a guide to managing your IP could be an important step for experienced authors to take. ALLi's *The Author Estate Book* and *The Author Heir Handbook*, available in the ALLi bookstore under Author Handbooks, can guide you through the process.

Although an experienced author can achieve many publishing opportunities by themselves, at a certain level, it makes sense to explore what rights could be better exploited by licensing IP. Receiving self-publishing commissions or publisher royalties is only one revenue stream for your books. There are many other possibilities, from translations to video games, merchandising to print. Translation rights are a current hot topic among successful authors wanting to open up new markets. But the rights world is a complex mix of formats, platforms, apps, territories, and terms, and each market and buyer offers different opportunities and operates by different rules. *How Authors Sell Publishing Rights* is ALLi's comprehensive guide to rights licensing, covering everything you need to begin successfully licensing your publishing rights. The guide is available in the online bookstore.

Work on making those mindset shifts toward being a more entrepreneurial author, and embrace the business side of your writing. It can be the difference between authors who are successful and those who wish they were. ■

Melissa Addey, Alli's Campaigns Manager

Melissa Addey

The Alliance of Independent Authors (ALLi) is a global membership association for self-publishing authors. A non-profit, our mission is ethics and excellence in self-publishing. Everyone on our team is a working indie author and we offer advice and advocacy for self-publishing authors within the literary, publishing and creative industries around the world. www.allianceindependentauthors.org

The January Slump

I've been in this business for more than eight years now. I've studied it and watched my own ups and downs. January is coming, and if you are exclusive to Amazon, then your page-read payout is most likely going to drop rather significantly.

The biggest names in the publishing world, both traditional and indie, sell vast numbers of books through the holidays. I know I do because those months have the highest payout rates, and I plan my publications and promotions that way. Those who can't buy will read in Kindle Unlimited because Amazon has shaped their product page to encourage Kindle Unlimited reading. "Read for Free" is the biggest button. A reader has to click underneath that button on a text link to become a buyer.

The rewards are clear for those who write compelling stories. The reader might not realize they borrowed a book instead of bought it, but when they start reading it and keep reading it, you as the author will see your page reads increase—especially during the fall publishing and promotions window.

I run sales on my omnibus editions and the first in most of my series during the October to December sales extravaganza. I am competing with traditional publishing houses who are also flooding the market with sales and new titles. You know what? With the best covers and great blurbs, my books do just fine. The stories within stand on their own, too, because I build up huge numbers of page reads during the fall promotion period.

It's a nice payday come the new year, but that winds down in January. Don't fight it. It is a fact of this business, but it's also a fact that your ad campaigns will become a whole lot cheaper in cost per click when the deep-pocket advertisers close their seasonal doors.

So I'll increase my advertising in January, and when my revenue bottoms out, it won't be bad at all. I expect it, but the good news is the windfall from the end of the previous year dampens the anguish of the January slump.

I also write new books during that time because I live in Alaska, where it's dark and cold in January and February. I mean really cold. Best to stay inside and set myself up to win in the spring when the rates climb once more—usually starting in February.

For reference, here are the KDP Select (Kindle Unlimited) payout rates since the program's inception: https://tinyurl.com/yv4maf2a. ■

Craig Martelle

Craig Martelle

High school Valedictorian enlists in the Marine Corps under a guaranteed tank contract. An inauspicious start that was quickly superseded by excelling in language study. Contract waived, a year at the Defense Language Institute to learn Russian and off to keep my ears on the big red machine during the Soviet years. Earned a four-year degree in two years by majoring in Russian Language. My general staff. career included choice side gigs - UAE, Bahrain, Korea, Russia, and Ukraine.

Major Martelle. I retired from the Marines after a couple years at the embassy in Moscow working arms control issues.

Department of Homeland Security then law school next. I was working for a high-end consulting firm performing business diagnostics, business law, and leadership coaching. For the money they paid me, I was good with that. Just until I wasn't. Then I started writing.

Dear Indie Annie,

I've always considered myself a planner, but my characters suddenly seem to have gone rogue! I can't figure out why my current story isn't working, but I'm in the middle of the series, so I can't really pivot either. How do I get this draft back in check before things go completely off the rails?

Outliner Out of My Depth

Dear Outliner,

I feel you so hard, my sweet child. Our precious characters can be willful devils sometimes, going rogue on us mid-story! But isn't that part of the fun? Take a zen breath—this is not a crisis but an opportunity for magic. Your word rebels are acting up because they have more to say. Time for a heart-to-heart chat with the little darlings.

I know you plotter types love your outlines, but stories are living things, not neatly plotted points! As a planner, you probably agree with Ursula K. Le Guin, who said, "The story—from prologue to epilogue—is a dangerous thing to get wrong, and cannot be allowed to drive itself." However, I would counter with the words of E. L. Doctorow: "Writing is like driving at night in the fog. You can only see as far as your headlights, but you can make the whole trip that way."

Even the best-laid plans go awry. Just ask Gandalf! Like the master wizard, Tolkien had to wrestle his characters into submission on many occasions. But deviation can reveal a story's soul. Embrace the unexpected. That makes the writing journey so magical. Surprising plot twists, unexpected character growth—this is where the story's heart beats.

Take Agatha Christie's *Miss Marple*. Christie knew the culprit from the start, but she let Miss Marple take the reins during the drafting. She followed her eccentric muse wherever she led!

Our characters' whims become the story's soul. Many authors "pants" their stories, following their characters and acting as a scribe along the way. Frightening

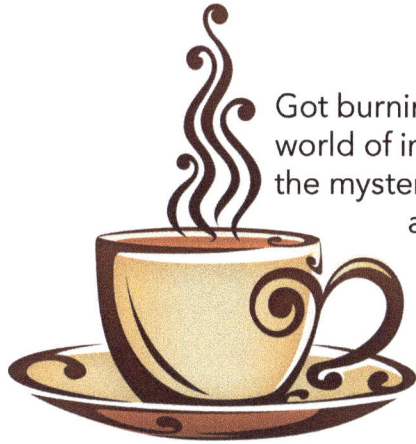

Got burning questions about the wibbly-wobbly world of indie authoring? Eager to unravel the mysteries of publishing, writing woes, or anything in between? Give your quizzical quills a whirl and shoot your musings over to indieannie@indieauthormagazine.com. Your inky quandaries are my cup of tea!

thought, eh? How dare your little darlings know better than you! Seriously though, I understand that with a deadline, careful plotting is advisable. As Anne Lamott says, give yourself the structure you need to guide the plot, but leave yourself some wiggle room for inspiration along the way.

Interestingly, she also writes: "Plot grows out of character. ...Over and over I feel as if my characters know who they are, and what happens to them...but they need me to write it down for them because their handwriting is so bad."

Now, about changing course mid-series: sometimes a new direction is needed if the story feels stale. But take care not to alienate your readership. It's not about reckless one-eighties. Make purposeful pivots.

Ask yourself: have you kept beloved elements like main characters that drew fans to the series? If so, you can safely introduce new settings, complications, or themes to refresh things—even to the point of dramatic character shifts if that development is logical or seems natural. When such developments stem from your characters living out their lives through you, then they should be.

If you are worried about how your audience will respond to these changes, share your creative process with your fans. Do you have ARC readers or a beta team you trust to give you honest, constructive feedback? Many writers share their works-in-progress with their readers as they write. Some even do this via a livestream on Facebook or YouTube. Personally, that would be a step too far for me and my natural modesty, but it is a great way to gauge how ideas will land with your fans, and they too can become part of the creative process. Alternatively, you could share a poll on social media or through your newsletter.

Put the outline aside for now. Listen to what your characters are trying to say. Let them lead you on an adventure. Loosen the reins a bit, and let your characters romp. Their breakout moments could take your story from good to extraordinary.

Once you complete this exploratory draft, then you can adjust things to align with your series arc if needed.

You've got this, sugar plum! Channel your inner Agatha and let those characters guide you, then polish the gems they reveal later. Your story is just waiting to be unearthed; now get writing and uncover its treasures!

Happy writing,
Indie Annie

X

10 TIPS FOR
INDIE AUTHOR TOOLS

In the heart of the indie author community, there is a particular writing group whose bond thrives on sharing knowledge and resources. Their connections formed over the course of a year as the members met at various events like the Smarter Artist Summit, 20Books Edinburgh, 20Books Vegas, and Mark Dawson's Self Publishing Show Live in London, and their bonds only grew stronger when the world went virtual in March 2020. Their daily virtual writing meetups and casual discussions on Facebook about projects, tools, and conferences led to a treasure trove of useful information. However, as the wealth of information grew, so did the need for a structured repository.

This necessity gave birth to IndieAuthorTools.com—a simple yet comprehensive platform created to house a growing database of tools, podcasts, software, courses, and other resources crucial for authors, and *IAM*'s sister site. Indie Author Tools is a place where authors can search for and compare service providers, be it cover designers, editors, or social media specialists. The database, available for free, also provides a catalog of tools, apps, podcasts, conferences, events, and books, serving as a one-stop toolbox for indie authors.

One cornerstone of IndieAuthorTools.com is the sense of community it fosters. Authors can connect with members, ask questions, and receive guidance from the support staff, making the self-publishing journey feel less daunting. The site also invites authors to contribute by suggesting their favorite tools or service providers, thus nurturing a community-driven platform where everyone can benefit.

Although registration is required for security reasons, access to the directory is free, and authors can choose to join with a pen name. Indie Author Tools is more than just a website; it's a collaborative effort by indie authors for indie authors, aiming to make the often solitary journey of writing and publishing a little less lonely and a lot more manageable.

Ready to explore it for yourself? Read on for *IAM*'s top tips for navigating and making the most of Indie Author Tools.

1 BROWSE THE COMPLETE DIRECTORY BY CATEGORY

Indie Author Tools offers a comprehensive directory categorized by various tools and resources, so indie authors can easily find what they need. Whether it's editing software, marketing platforms, or publishing services, an organized directory saves time and can introduce authors to new tools they might not have discovered otherwise.

2 CHAT WITH AN INTERACTIVE LIBRARIAN

A standout feature on IndieAuthorTools.com is the interactive librarian, a chatbot engineered to assist the indie author community. The chatbot has been trained on all the tools listed on the site, articles from *Indie Author Magazine*, and the training courses featured on Author Tech Summit, so it can provide specific answers to authors' individual questions. Unlike other AI models, the librarian also doesn't feed any other generative large language model (LLM); it operates in a closed model, ensuring a tailored and secure interaction exclusive to indie authors and devoid of external influences from other AI models. It's about creating a reliable and tailored resource, making the vast world of self-publishing a bit more navigable for indie authors.

3 REVIEW TOOLS

Before investing time and resources into a new tool, it's wise to see what others have experienced. On IndieAuthorTools.com, each tool listed has a review feature that allows fellow authors to leave their honest feedback in the form of a written review and/or star ratings on several aspects of the experience. This section unveils real-world insights into a tool's usability, effectiveness, and value, which can serve as a valuable aid for authors making informed decisions.

But it's not just a one-way street of information. Companies providing the tools also can respond to inquiries and reviews. Authors can have their concerns or questions addressed directly by the companies, and the companies can provide additional information, clarify functionalities, or offer support.

4 SUGGEST AN APP OR YOUR FAVORITE COURSE

If you have a favorite tool that's not listed, suggesting an app can help grow the directory and aid other authors in finding useful tools. It's a straightforward way to contribute to the community and share valuable resources.

Authors can share and discover courses that can help hone writing, marketing, or publishing skills. Sharing educational resources can provide immense value to the community, helping authors at all levels to improve their craft and marketing efforts.

5 FIND A NEW PODCAST

Among the categories of tools authors can find on the site is one specifically for writing- and publishing-focused podcasts. Those featured in the database cover a range of topics from writing techniques to the business side of self-publishing. Find the current collection by navigating to the Search by Category tab on the homepage and selecting "Podcasts."

6 SIGN UP FOR THE WEEKLY EMAIL

If you're hoping to browse the resources available rather than looking for a specific tool, Indie Author Tools' weekly email is a convenient way to stay updated on the latest tools, articles, podcasts, and other resources. It's designed to keep authors in the loop in the ever-evolving indie author landscape without having to check for updates constantly.

7 CATCH UP ON INDIE ANNIE'S LATEST ARTICLE

Frequent *IAM* readers will recognize everyone's favorite advice-giving indie aunt in the magazine's pages each month, but Indie Annie makes an appearance on the Indie Author Tools database as well. Each month's letter answers a real author's question about the world of independent publishing—with just a hint of Annie's signature sass. Visitors can read through her latest letter on the site or browse previous articles that cover trending topics, provide tips, and share experiences to benefit other indie authors via the Dear Indie Annie tab on the homepage.

8 LIST OR CLAIM YOUR OWN TOOL OR BUSINESS

For those who've developed a tool or run a business beneficial to indie authors, listing or claiming it on the Indie Author Tools platform can help reach a wider audience. If your tool or service is already listed, hit the "Claim Listing" button beneath the description. If you need to submit a new listing, you can find the "List Tool or Service" button in the top right corner of the homepage.

Pro Tip: Simple listings are free, but you can also include more detailed business information with a Silver or Gold advertising subscription. Silver level subscriptions cost $10 per month, and Gold level subscriptions cost $20 per month.

9 ADD TO THE CONFERENCE CALENDAR

Know of an event coming up that you want other authors to hear about, or are you looking to sprinkle some excitement into your plans for next year? The conference calendar allows you to stay updated on upcoming conferences, workshops, and events. Find it at https://indieauthortools.com/conferences.

---

10 FIND YOUR NEW FAVORITE BOOK

One of the cornerstone features of IndieAuthorTools.com is its extensive books section, housing over two hundred titles curated for indie authors. The collection ranges from specific guides tailored for indie authors, like mastering MailerLite or optimizing Amazon ads, to broader topics, from prominent business authors teaching essential skills such as time management and productivity. It's a well-rounded library designed to cater to the diverse needs of the indie author community.

What sets this section apart is the review process. Indie Author Tools editors review each submission, ensuring any books featured maintain a level of quality and relevance to the indie author journey. This isn't a stagnant list; new books are added each month, keeping the resource fresh and up-to-date with the evolving landscape of self-publishing.

IndieAuthorTools.com aims to serve as a practical guidepost in the expansive journey of self-publishing. Created by indie authors, for indie authors, it embodies a straightforward mission: to streamline the path from manuscript to published work by providing a merged platform for tools, resources, and community interaction. In the self-publishing arena, where new tools and resources sprout continually, having a go-to platform that not only lists these resources but also provides a space for authors to share their experiences is invaluable.

Whether you're a newcomer to the indie author scene or a seasoned writer, IndieAuthorTools.com offers a space to learn, share, and grow. And while the act of writing may be a solitary endeavor, this platform reminds us that the journey towards publishing and marketing your work is a collaborative adventure. ■

Chelle Honiker

Chelle Honiker

As the publisher of Indie Author Magazine, Chelle Honiker brings nearly three decades of startup, technology, training, and executive leadership experience to the role. She's a serial entrepreneur, founding and selling multiple successful companies including a training development company, travel agency, website design and hosting firm, a digital marketing consultancy, and a wedding planning firm. She's organized and curated multiple TEDx events and hired to assist other nonprofit organizations as a fractional executive, including The Travel Institute and The Freelance Association.

As a writer, speaker, and trainer she believes in the power of words and their ability to heal, inspire, incite, and motivate. Her greatest inspiration is her daughters, Kelsea and Cathryn, who tolerate her tendency to run away from home to play with her friends around the world for months at a time. It's said she could run a small country with just the contents of her backpack.

Rebel with a Cause

SACHA BLACK BUILDS HER AUTHOR CAREER ON AUTHENTICITY, HELPING OTHER WRITERS

Who knew growing up in a remote village in the UK would be the spark that started a young woman's journey to authorship?

Such was the case for Sacha Black, podcast host, content and communication strategist for the Alliance of Independent Authors (ALLi), and self-defined writing rebel. Sacha's role in the author community is multifaceted, but those facets have helped her shine brightly within the author community. Last week, she was gracious enough to have a chat with me, where I learned what made her who she is today and where she envisions the publishing field heading in 2024.

EARLY ON

As most future authors probably do, Sacha read a lot as a child, but in her small village, she found an equally small library. Eventually, she grew tired of reading the same books, and her parents had to drive her to a nearby library that was bigger so she could have more choices.

Later, she studied at university, earning a master's degree in psychology and another in public management, with plans to pursue a PhD and enter academia. She says she quickly discovered that this wasn't the path for her, but around the same time, she had been blogging—rather, drinking wine and blogging, she clari-

fies—and naturally fell into a writing community as a result. The experience taught her how to write, and she shared her lessons learned on her blog, with "lots of dick jokes and swearing," she says.

Sacha also explored a bit of the writing market at the time and found a limited supply of craft books on villains. Given her interest in the topic, she decided to write the book herself. That book, published in 2017, was titled *13 Steps to Evil: How to Craft Superbad Villains*. She sold eighty-seven copies, she says, and is proud to admit it. Throughout our conversation, she spoke humbly, and we shared how and where we each got our start. A lot has changed since then.

Today, Sacha says she's focusing more on her fiction prose, which amounts to nearly seventeen published novels in YA Fantasy and Sapphic Fantasy. She also boasts five books on writing craft, which include topics such as writing compelling heroes and villains. But writing isn't the only corner of the indie author world where she's found a home.

PATREON AND THE REBEL AUTHOR PODCAST

Sacha seems determined to carve out her little corner of the publishing industry. Alongside her own writing, she is the host of the *Rebel Author Podcast*, where she's cleared over two hundred episodes alongside industry guests, covering topics such as writing craft, marketing, and publishing news.

Sacha says her Patreon page meshes well with the podcast—they fuel each other. On her Patreon, Sacha will pick a book and

dissect it, from the prose to the structure, pacing, and more. Then, she and her Patreon group will discuss what they've discovered, and she'll give her own unique take on it in a podcast episode, a sort of mini lesson on the book. She says the group allows her to have a sense of community and a chance to share and learn about writing together.

On her end, Sacha says she makes sure she provides valuable insight into what works or doesn't work, slipping in kernels of knowledge about marketing and advertising along the way. She was candid and quick to let me know that she too had to learn how to be a great writer—and that she will never stop learning.

Outside of her podcast, Sacha shares the knowledge she's amassed through courses and consulting. She's also a guest speaker and has appeared at 20BooksTo50K® events and the London Book Fair. I asked at one point if she had any plans to use her graduate studies in psychology in her career. She laughed and said she does, only now, she applies what she learned at university to a field she loves.

ALLIANCE OF INDEPENDENT AUTHORS

ALLi is an international nonprofit organization that values ethics and excellence in self-publishing. The group advocates on behalf of independent authors, guiding them with knowledge to help them selectively license their publishing rights, give contract advice, and provide much-needed advice in an ever-changing field.

There seems to be a shared vision between Sacha and ALLi—that of helping authors from all walks of life succeed. Sacha's close involvement with the organization makes sense, then. She started off as a blog manager and conference organizer and says she was enthralled at the opportunities she had to campaign on behalf of indie authors. Later, as her own writing developed, she took on a more nuanced role as ALLi's content and communications strategist. She still works with the organization today, but her current role allows her to focus on more high-level strategies for delivering ALLi's message to the masses.

ONE LESSON TO SHARE

Near the end of the conversation, I put Sacha in a box and asked her to share one piece of advice for new authors—some amalgamation of all she has learned. I had the treat of watching her wrack her brain for a way to summarize what had to be a treasure trove of knowledge.

"Find the unique thing about you," she finally said. "That's when you're most authentic, and that's when you'll find your tribe and connect to readers and find success."

I started to see a greater vision of what Sacha teaches her audience: authenticity above all else, community with other authors and readers, and to capitalize on what makes you unique. For Sacha, it's in the name of her podcast, the *Rebel Author*, where she says you can find "books, business, and bad words."

EYES ON THE FUTURE

Before parting, I threw out a question to Sacha, wanting to know where she saw publishing heading in 2024 given she regularly keeps a pulse on the industry.

Sacha says she's been in the indie author community since 2013, and right now, it feels like the blue waters of that time. She says she believes direct sales will be the next frontier, and there will be a focus on higher quality products. She writes in a small, hungry niche, and feeding them what they are looking for is getting easier and easier, she says. Sacha's goals for now are to focus on her small, dedicated family in her Patreon group—her nonfiction community—and, otherwise, to try to be more human.

We can all take a few lessons from Sacha, things that not only she has said but other industry professionals have as well. Focus on community, remain authentic, and always try to improve your craft. If you do those things, you'll "find your tribe and your readers, and find success," Sacha says. ■

David Viergutz

David Viergutz

David Viergutz is a disabled Army Veteran, Law Enforcement Veteran, husband and proud father. He is an author of stories from every flavor of horror and dark fiction. One day, David's wife sat him down and gave him the confidence to start putting his imagination on paper. From then on out his creativity has no longer been stifled by self-doubt and he continues to write with a smile on his face in a dark, candle-lit room.

Photo courtesy of Elaine Bateman

Success in the Subarctic:
A LOOK BACK AT THE 2022 INDIE CAPSTONE EVENT IN FAIRBANKS, ALASKA

It had been half a year in the making since Craig Martelle, co-founder of 20BooksTo50K®, began inviting authors from around the world, promising a unique experience that would challenge and reward them. Following the success of the first Indie Capstone event in Las Vegas early in the year, Martelle promised a new group of authors who were willing to invest in themselves and their future a chance to take their author businesses to the next level, to break free of the limitations of their own imaginations, and to find a new level of success.

So on a crisp October morning in 2022, a small group of authors gathered at a hotel in Fairbanks, Alaska.

Unlike the thousand-person-strong 20Books conferences, Martelle's Indie Capstone events are small, private weekend retreats that are designed to help authors grow and level up in their publishing careers. Each two-day event is designed to include space for all aspects of an indie author's business—not just craft or marketing but also how to shift focus between them. With five-minute writing sprints, formal sessions, and Q&As packing the schedule, they're also designed so authors at virtually any stage of their careers can benefit.

Despite the long flights, the mood ahead of the 2022 capstone was one of pure excitement. Everyone was eager to see what Martelle had in store for them, and he didn't disappoint. He delivered an in-depth workshop on writing and marketing, where he shared tips and advice from his years of experience as an indie author. The attending authors discussed successful strategies they had used in their own careers, providing valuable insight into what works best.

I asked Sarah Blackard, who writes clean Romantic Suspense and Rom-Com, about her best takeaway. "Sometimes it's just little tweaks that can make a really big difference in your author business," she says. "There are so many different genres represented here. Having this intimate environment makes it really good to learn tidbits that you can take home and put into action."

Todd Fahnestock, an author of Epic Fantasy, described having a breakthrough moment about advertising over the course of the weekend. "There were a whole lot of small details that really opened my mind and made it suddenly accessible to do what I've been lacking all this time. That was huge for me. That's what I came for and that's what I got, and the rest is all gravy as far as I'm concerned."

Everyone had a list of things they planned to do differently going forward. Terry Wells-Brown, writer of Romantic Suspense, Sexy Thriller, and Contemporary Fantasy, was no exception. "I'm planning a complete revamping of my business and how I manage my readers," she says. "Indie Capstone has made a huge impact on me."

Alec Peche, author of twenty Mystery and Thriller books, was also excited to be getting on with her new to-do list. "It's been incredibly valuable

34 | Indie Author Magazine ·Issue 32

to me. I learned some things about Amazon ads that I didn't realize. I've got a list of tactics to go home with, to improve my reader engagement."

Alex Bates writes material for role-playing games. He's also written a couple of comic books and had some Science Fiction short stories published. "I'd say that today the biggest value I got was out of the group discussion led by Craig, where we really narrowed in on and delineated our goals specifically," he said at the event. "I knew what my goals were generally before this, but with a group of like-minded people like this who are all in various stages of the trip that I'm on, it was really helpful to be able to pinpoint specific things that I needed to focus on."

In the intimate setting, people seemed willing to speak more freely. Bates explained, "The information that Craig and some of the others have shared has been incredibly useful. Having people to bounce ideas and concepts off of, and hearing what's worked for some people and hasn't worked for others, and that ability to compare, and pick and choose what might work for us, has been so useful."

But it's not all about the learning. Making connections is its own reward. Lolo Page writes Romantic Suspense and Romantic Comedies. "I love being at Indie Capstone," she said. "I made so many friends here. It's always good to talk with authors, other writers. My battery was running low after hard-charging words for the first six months of this year, and I needed to recharge and get with my people to help me figure out how to move forward. Indie Capstone, for me, has forced me to zero in on what is important, what I need to do right away to rein in my time management so that I can increase my revenue and my output. And for that, I'm thankful."

Even those who were already on the right track found their time in Fairbanks had been well worth it. Lori Matthews writes Romantic Suspense. I asked what she would advise anybody thinking about coming to an Indie Capstone. "They really should," she answered. "It's amazing to get the collective energy from all the other writers in the room. It feeds the well and makes you feel so good to be with your people. It's just a nice check-in to be with all the people that are just like you. It really has been worth it in every way. I am doing what I should be

doing and will firm up what I'm working on. I have a couple of things to revisit, but it's nice to know that I am on the right path."

The authors left Alaska with a greater understanding of the publishing process, a broader network of support, and even some new friendships that they were certain would last long beyond that October gathering.

This attendee had only one disappointment during October's event—I arrived with a furry hat and snow-proof boots but there wasn't a flake of snow to be found. But Fairbanks has a lot to offer between its excellent Thai food, of which it's the capital outside Thailand, and a natural hot springs resort just out of town.

The fourth Indie Capstone is set to take place March 16 and 17, 2024, with attendees to be selected by Martelle from a pool of applicants. The cost, excluding travel expenses, runs about $500 per person. As for those who've already ventured to the US's northernmost state, the lessons learned and the connections made by October 2022's attendees still resonate. Martelle's publishing retreat offered an amazing experience, and—lack of snow notwithstanding—future Indie Capstones are sure to live up to the legacy. ◾

Elaine Bateman

Elaine Bateman

In her pre-author life, Elaine worked for FTSE 100 and Fortune 500 companies in procurement, project support, and IT Training. She has a bachelor of science. in Systems Practice and Design.

Everyone Wants to Be A Mogul

GUEST AUTHOR RUSSELL NOHELTY EXAMINES THE TRANSMEDIA TREND IN THE INDIE AUTHOR WORLD

There's genre hopping, and then there's medium hopping.

Depending on how you look at his career, Russell Nohelty has done both. As a *USA Today* bestselling author and the co-founder of Writer MBA and the Author Ecosystem archetypes, Nohelty has put his name on graphic novels, Fantasy novels, nonfiction author guides, and more. At the same time, he's created card games and comics, collaborated with a coffee brand, and explored a range of other areas seemingly far outside of the literary world. It's all in an effort to capitalize on the growing trend of utilizing transmedia—expanding a story across multiple mediums to draw in new audiences.

Transmedia is not an adaptation of a story; instead, it's the use of various mediums to explore new aspects of an existing story world. It's also part of the future of the indie author industry, Nohelty says. This month, Nohelty is sharing his thoughts on the concept, the benefits and challenges it can pose for authors, and—most importantly—how authors can use transmedia to grow their readership and their business.

Living in Los Angeles, some of the most common questions I get revolve around how to turn a book into a movie, video game, or generally how to translate an author's work into another medium.

Transmedia is definitely a buzzword, but it doesn't mean what you think it means. It's not about translating your existing work into a new format verbatim. It's much cooler—and more complicated.

From a production standpoint, transmedia storytelling involves creating content that engages an audience using various techniques to permeate their daily lives. To achieve this engagement, a transmedia production will develop stories across multiple forms of media in order to deliver unique pieces of content on each channel. Importantly, these pieces of content are not only linked, overtly or subtly, but they are also in narrative synchronization with one another.

My current understanding of transmedia is that it involves telling a cohesive story across mediums. And one of my favorite examples is *Matrix: Reloaded*.

I love *Matrix: Reloaded*, despite all the hate it receives, but I will admit that a lot of my love for that movie comes from the *Enter the Matrix* video game. You learn so much more about the world of the movie by playing the game.

Another example is *The Lizzie Bennet Diaries*, wherein the YouTube series was augmented by Twitter feeds and other media that fleshed out the world.

The goal of a transmedia project is to find new audiences for your work by expanding formats to capture new fans across modalities. In authorship, this is expressed perfectly by the LitRPG genre. Authors combined role-playing games and novels into one story to bring in fans from each and create something wholly new.

Of course, LitRPGs are not transmedia; they are multimodal. If you talk to a LitRPG author for any length of time, they will start talking about modalities, which are the specific ways that something is experienced or expressed. So why am I confusing you by talking about LitRPG when it's not even an example of transmedia? Because thinking in modalities is a key feature of having success in transmedia.

With transmedia, the author's job is to express ideas in new and exciting ways that will drive new readers to your books. To have success with transmedia, you need to stop thinking about your books as the end product and pull back to focus on your brand as a whole.

If you're interested in transmedia, here are four options with a relatively low barrier to entry:

- **Choose-your-own-adventure blog:** It's relatively cheap, though time-consuming, to set up a blog with a branching decision tree set in your universe.
- **Augmented reality social media profiles:** If you have a contemporary story, you can set up social media profiles that flush out your world.
- **One-page RPG adventure:** While creating an entire RPG is time-consuming and expensive, building a one-page RPG that can be consumed easily is manageable with limited resources.
- **A website for a business in your world:** With all the website builders on the market today, it's relatively simple and cheap to set up a website that helps draw people into your work.

There are countless more simple and effective ways to draw readers deeper into your brand. However, each will still have a financial and mental cost. This is why most authors working in transmedia rely heavily on partnerships to succeed. If an author can find a partner and trust them to carry out their vision, then they can grow exponentially.

Attracting partners usually takes a successful series with significant success behind it. Look at George Lucas. He had the most popular movies in the world with the Star Wars series, which allowed him to release merchandising and create other media quickly to feed his fandom.

For years, the brand only had three movies. But if movies were the primary modality by which people found his work, people funneled to and from the movies into toy lines, video games, television shows, books, comics, and more. Lucas primarily grew his brand by expressing his vision through modalities outside of movies, and through characters in his universe who weren't in the core cast.

This is the ideal way to think about having success in transmedia. The question is really, "How can I bring new fans of my work by engaging with them in a new way?"

Earlier this year, I worked with a company to release a card game for one of my brands, and I'm working with different companies to create other experiences that allow my existing fans to express their excitement in new ways while bringing new fans into my universe. Whatever you choose to do, the goal is to meet fans where they are and introduce them to your universe in new and interesting ways.

On top of that, you give your existing fans more ways to fall deeper in love with your brand.

Just a quick note of warning: once you start "feeding the beast" and expanding your brand, fans in those new modalities will expect you to continue servicing their needs, which can be expensive. Additionally, while you likely know how to grow your readership, every time you enter a new market, you are effectively starting from scratch. Yes, you might have fans willing to join you in other modalities, but you might not.

Reaching out to brand partners can be scary, but brands, especially newer ones, are looking for established brands they can partner with in order to grow their own audiences. There are likely already new and emerging companies in the modalities you are looking to explore that would be interested in working with you, if you have sales and an audience to back up your enthusiasm.

This is one reason doubling down on learning sales and marketing is so important. Once you have sales behind your series, brand partners will come out of the woodwork to work with you.

Last year we had a coffee brand reach out to us to launch a *Cthulhu is Hard to Spell* decaf coffee, and it was great. If you don't have the sales to justify expansion yet, the best thing you can do is learn how to sell your books so that you have an audience that attracts brands to you while also giving you an audience to serve.

None of these modalities will likely be a silver bullet to make you a fortune alone, but bring them together, and you can create a compelling universe that fans want to live in for years to come. ◾

Russell Nohelty

Russell Nohelty

Russell Nohelty is a *USA Today* bestselling author. He is the co-founder of the Author Ecosystem archetypes that help authors embrace their natural sales and marketing tendencies to have sustained success. You can take the quiz to find your ecosystem at authorecosystem.com.

The Indie Author's Guide for Navigating Contracts as a Small Business Owner

As small business owners, indie authors deal with a lot of contracts—both those we need to sign and, in some cases, those we create. Whether it's a collaboration with a coauthor, hiring an editor or cover designer, or tied to an event you're planning to attend, contracts are a vital part of our professional journey. Yet, all too often, we skim through these documents without truly understanding what we're signing.

As tedious as they can seem, it is vital that you read contracts thoroughly in order to understand the terms and conditions of the agreement, protect your interests, and avoid potential legal and financial consequences. In this article, we'll explore the significance of understanding contracts and provide insights into how to navigate them effectively, giving you the knowledge and confidence you need to protect your rights as a creator.

THE IMPORTANCE OF UNDERSTANDING CONTRACTS

Contracts are the backbone of any business, and the indie author's career is no exception. These legally binding agreements govern the terms of engagement, responsibilities, and expectations of a business agreement, and they can significantly impact your writing journey. Here's why understanding contracts is crucial:

- **Legal Protection:** Contracts safeguard your rights and interests. They clarify roles and responsibilities, payment terms, deadlines, and more. In case of any disputes, a well-structured contract can protect your work and your income.
- **Professionalism:** Taking the time to understand and create clear, comprehensive contracts demonstrates professionalism. It ensures transparency in your business relationships and builds trust with collaborators, editors, or designers.
- **Risk Mitigation:** Contracts can help you identify and address potential issues in advance. By specifying what happens in various scenarios, you can avoid misunderstandings and complications down the road.
- **Empowerment:** Understanding contracts empowers you to negotiate favorable terms and make informed decisions. You can ensure that the agreement aligns with your goals and values as an author.

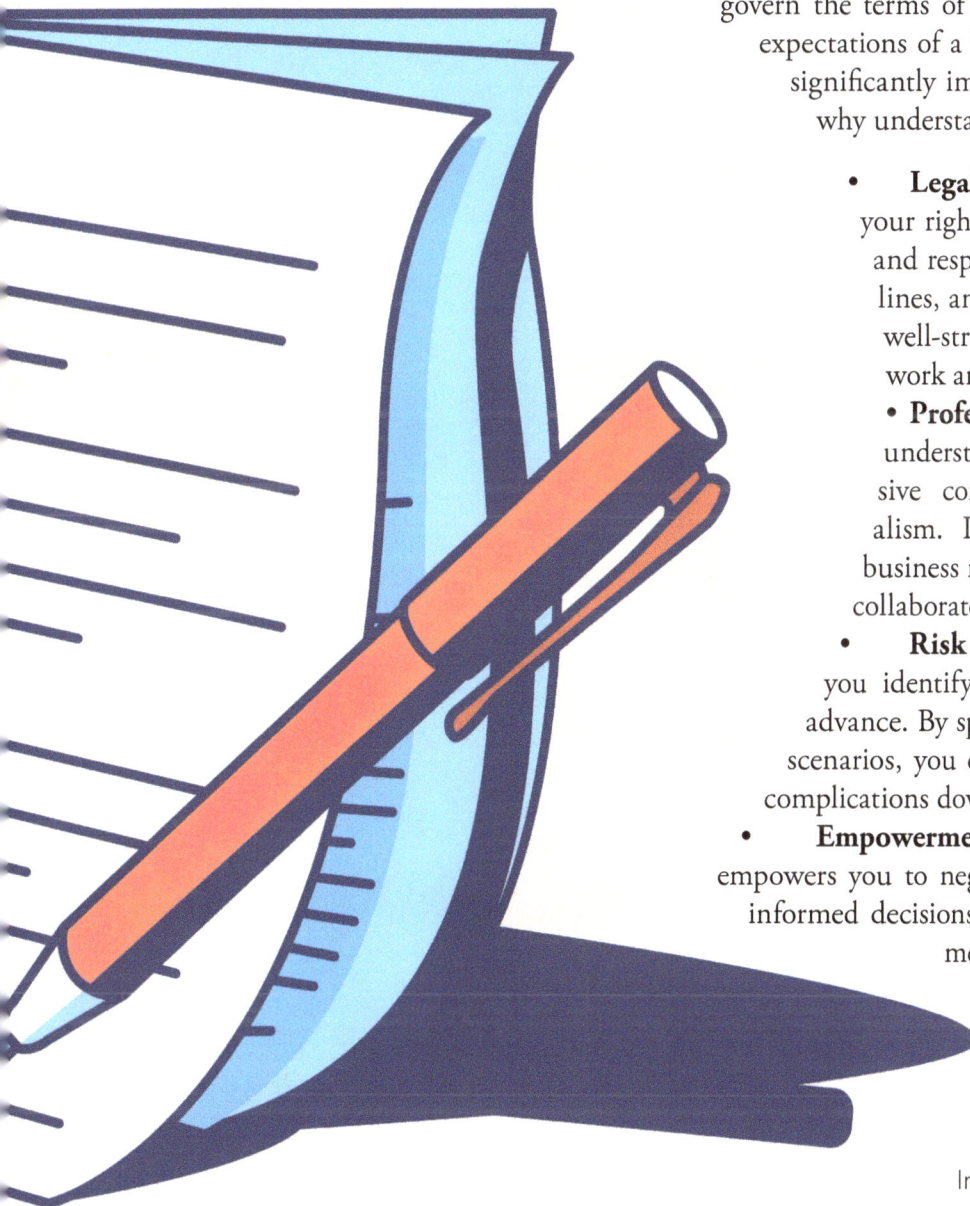

TRANSLATING LEGALESE: A GUIDE TO UNDERSTANDING CONTRACTS AND AVOIDING RED FLAGS

When you receive a contract, it is crucial to take the time to read it carefully. Contracts are complex legal documents, and the language used may not always be straightforward. By dedicating sufficient time to comprehending the entire contract, you gain a clear understanding of its significance and context. This ensures that you're fully aware of what you're committing to.

Payment terms are often one of the most critical aspects of a contract. They specify when and how much money is to be exchanged. Pay close attention to these provisions to make sure they align with your expectations and financial capabilities. For example, are there penalties for late payments? Are there installment plans? Are there any conditions for invoicing?

Contracts often have time-sensitive elements. You need to be aware of deadlines for deliverables, project completion, or any other time-bound obligations. Missing these deadlines can have serious consequences, so understanding and planning for them is essential.

If the contract involves intellectual property, such as content creation or creative work, pay careful attention to the copyright provisions. Understanding who retains ownership of the intellectual property and any licensing or usage rights is crucial. This can impact your ability to use or monetize your work in the future. Ensure any contract you sign clearly defines who holds the rights to the work and how royalties will be distributed, and for how long those rights are retained.

Confidentiality clauses are vital in many contracts, especially in business and employment agreements. These clauses outline both your and the other party's responsibility to protect sensitive information and trade secrets. Misunderstanding or violating these clauses can lead to legal liabilities and reputational damage.

Dispute resolution clauses dictate how conflicts between the parties should be handled. Some contracts require mediation or arbitration before pursuing legal action, while others may specify the jurisdiction for legal proceedings. Understanding this aspect is essential, as it can affect how you address disagreements or conflicts in the future.

When reviewing contracts, be on the lookout for certain clauses or phrases that could have a significant impact on your author career. The language used in contracts can be technical and legalistic, making it easy to misread or misunderstand the intended meaning. Paying special attention to these

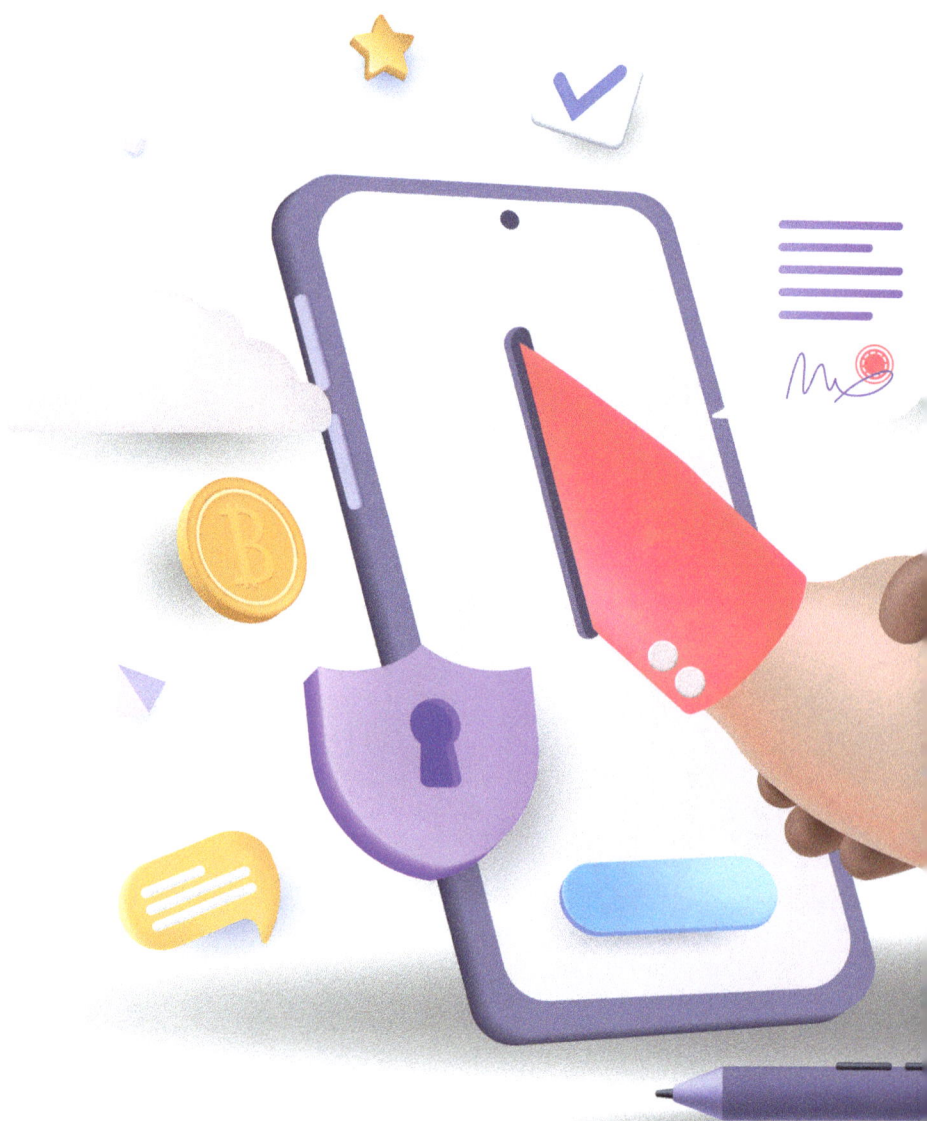

sections helps prevent such misinterpretations and can identify potential issues so you can address them ahead of time.

Pro Tip: The Alliance of Independent Authors (ALLi) offers a glossary that enables you to understand the parts of a contract and the legal terms you're most likely to encounter as an indie author: https://selfpublishingadvice.org/contracts-for-indie-authors-a-glossary. ALLi members can also reach out to the nonprofit's legal team for advice on specific contracts.

ADDRESSING UNWANTED CLAUSES

If you encounter clauses or phrases you don't agree with in a contract from an editor or designer, it's crucial to communicate your concerns. Discuss the terms with the other party and consider negotiating changes that better align with your needs and expectations. Flexibility and open communication can lead to more favorable agreements for both parties. And remember, in almost any situation, the contract signee can ask for amendments or additions if needed.

Understanding contracts is a fundamental aspect of managing your author career. These legal agreements play a pivotal role in protecting your rights, maintaining professionalism, and mitigating risks. By mastering the art of contract negotiation and comprehension, indie authors can navigate their careers with confidence and safeguard their creative work.

CREATING YOUR OWN CONTRACTS

If you work with virtual assistants (VAs), coauthors, or other collaborators, you may need to create your own contracts. These documents should cover key aspects of your working relationship, such as responsibilities, payment terms, and deadlines. It's essential to be specific and clear in your contracts, leaving no room for ambiguity.

While there are plenty of boilerplate contracts available online or through professional organizations like the Authors Guild (https://authorsguild.org) or ALLi, not all will be tailored to self-publishing authors or to the specific agreement you're entering.

By creating your own custom agreement based on your needs as an indie author—whether that's retaining all rights while still allowing others limited usage permissions; setting clear deadlines without sacrificing creative freedom; or ensuring fair compensation rates no matter how successful sales become—you can rest easy knowing everything has

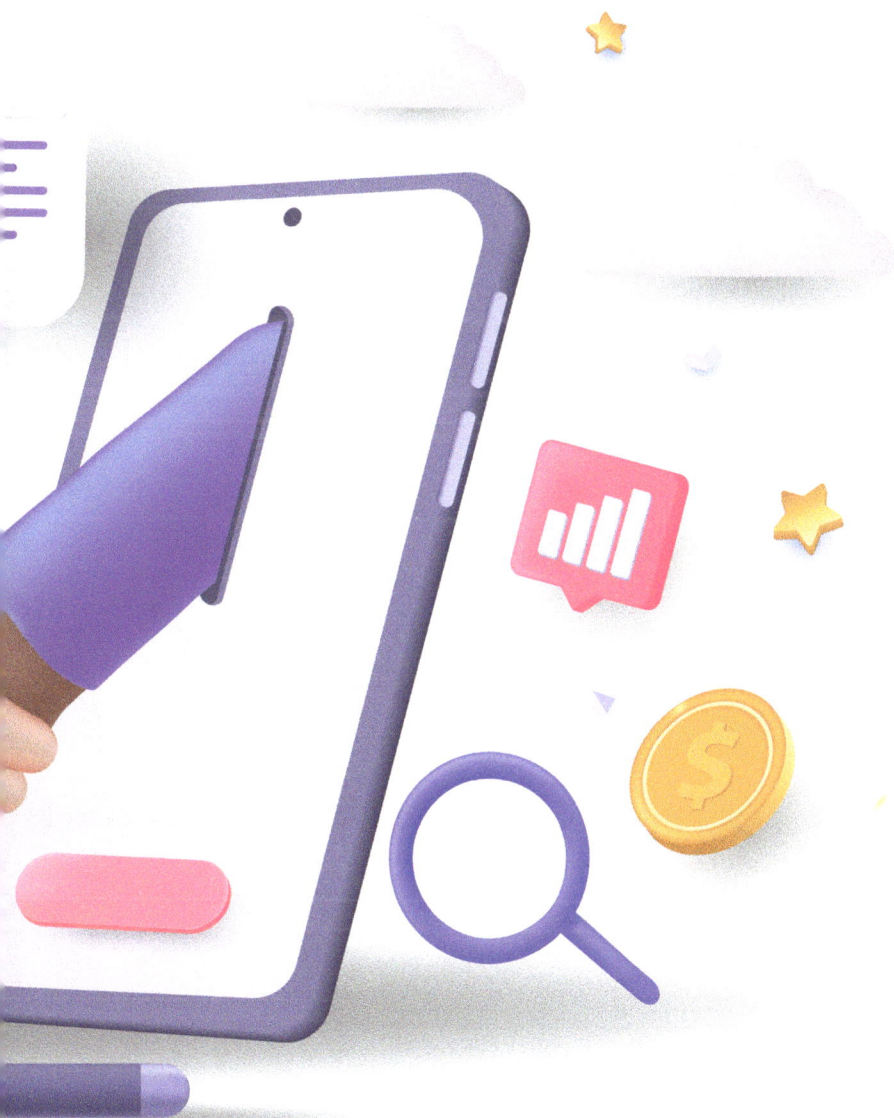

been spelled out clearly upfront before any money changes hands.

Here are six steps to follow when creating your own contract:

1. **Identify the parties and define the relationship.** Clearly state the names and contact information—this means legal names, not just pen names or trading names—of all parties involved, and define the nature of the relationship, whether it's for services, collaborations, or partnerships.

2. **Outline the scope of work.** Provide a detailed description of the services or responsibilities each party will undertake, being sure to specify deliverables, timelines, and any other relevant expectations.

3. **Include payment terms**, such as the amount, due dates, and payment methods. Address intellectual property rights, specifying who owns what and whether any licenses are granted. Establish confidentiality clauses to protect sensitive information. Define dispute resolution mechanisms in case of conflicts. Specify termination conditions and notice periods, if applicable. Finally, address any warranties, guarantees, or indemnification clauses.

4. **Define responsibilities and obligations.** Clearly outline each party's roles and responsibilities. Specify any limitations on these responsibilities, if necessary. For example, an author may acknowledge that they are solely responsible for the accuracy and factual correctness of the content. The editor's role may be limited to grammar, spelling, and style, with no responsibility for fact-checking.

5. **Consider local and national laws.** Ensure your contract complies with applicable local, state, and national laws. If your contract involves international parties, consider relevant international laws as well. The privacy laws for the European Union offer an obvious example for authors selling their books in Europe. The General Data Protection Regulation (GDPR) imposes significant responsibilities on businesses and provides strong enforcement mechanisms to ensure compliance. In any case, it can be a good idea to consult with legal counsel to tailor the contract to your specific needs, as legal requirements can vary depending on the jurisdiction and the nature of the agreement.

6. **Review, revise, and seek legal advice if necessary.** Carefully review your contract to ensure clarity and completeness, and edit it as needed to address any concerns or requirements you or your collaborator highlight. If your contract is complex or high-stakes,

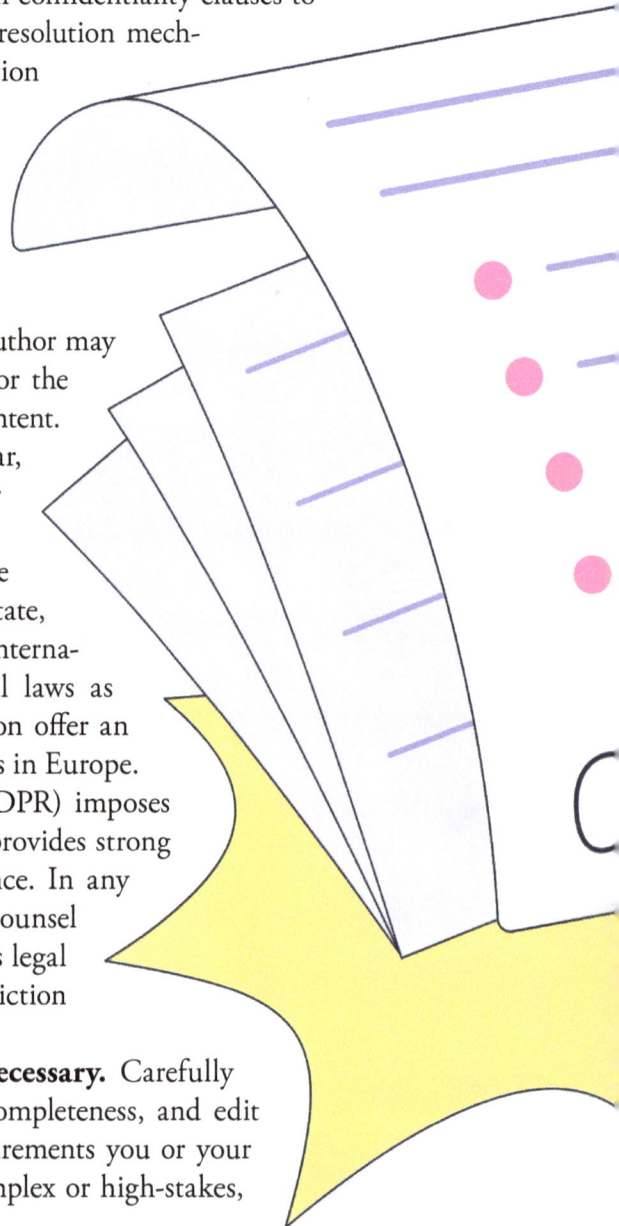

consider seeking legal advice to ensure that it offers maximum protection and aligns with your interests.

If you are unsure about any part of a contract, be it one you've received or one you have created, consider seeking legal advice, either with an attorney or through a professional author service such as

- ALLi (https://allianceindependentauthors.org);
- the Authors Guild (https://authorsguild.org);
- the Society of Authors (https://www2.societyofauthors.org);
- the Australian Society of Authors (https://asauthors.org.au);
- or other industry organizations.

Remember that contract creation can vary depending on the specific context and legal requirements of a business. It's essential to tailor your contract to the unique needs and circumstances of the parties involved. When in doubt, consulting with an attorney experienced in the relevant field can provide valuable guidance and help you create a legally sound contract.

Contracts protect your rights and ensure that you receive fair compensation for your hard work. By understanding the basics of agreements, you can avoid costly mistakes and make informed decisions that will benefit you in the long run. Knowledge is power! Take the time to educate yourself on the different types of agreements, and seek professional help if necessary.

Remember, as an indie author, you have the power to control your career and achieve success on your terms. Don't let a poorly written contract stand in your way. ■

Tanya Nellestein

Tanya Nellestein

Tanya Nellestein is an avid reader, experience enthusiast, outstanding car vocalist, and Queen of fancy dress. In her spare time she is also a bestselling and award-winning author and journalist with a penchant for bloodthirsty battles and steamy romance. From Vikings to present day, Tanya writes page-turning, gut-churning stories with a romantic angle that always includes good sex and a happily ever after - eventually. Her debut novel, The Valkyrie's Viking recently hit Amazon's best seller list and her sixth novel, This Side of Fate, was the 2022 winner of the Romance Writers of Australia Sapphire Award for Best Unpublished Romance Manuscript. In 2021, Tanya won the Romance Writers of Australia Romance in Media Award. Tanya lives on the outskirts of Sydney, Australia amidst a cavalcade of never ending disasters, both natural and those of her own making.

Build Your Perfect AI Assistant with These ChatGPT Plug-Ins for Writers

Over the past year, we've seen artificial intelligence and generative language models explode in popularity and capability. ChatGPT, developed by OpenAI, saw close to 1.7 billion visits to the site in October, according to Similarweb. Although the ethics of the programs remain hotly debated in many circles, including in the indie author community, many industries are continuing to explore potential uses for AI as a time- and energy-saving tool.

Of course, as users have been learning the programs, the programs have been learning as well. Even if AI programs like ChatGPT seemed somewhat limited in scope initially, as more people use them, the programs continue to gather additional training data and develop higher-quality outputs. But those aren't the only ways the programs can grow. Thanks to plug-ins, it's easy for individual users to broaden the platforms, customizing the tools to better suit their needs.

WHAT IS A PLUG-IN?

Plug-ins are pieces of software that add new features or extend the functionality of an existing application. Plug-ins are extensions that integrate with software or websites, meaning you won't need to exit the application to access the additional features. The application's developer and others with programming knowledge generally can create plug-ins of their own, though the ability to do so varies from program to program, but users don't need to have a programming background to use them.

For authors wanting to use AI in their businesses, plug-ins can open the doors to entirely new creative opportunities. Read on to explore several ChatGPT plug-ins tailored to writing and publishing and evaluate their ease of use, benefits, and potential drawbacks.

THE BASICS

To use plug-ins on ChatGPT, you must be subscribed to ChatGPT Plus, which costs $20 a month. ChatGPT Plus also grants you access to GPT-4, OpenAI's newest large language model. After subscribing, you can select "Plug-ins (Beta)" from the pop-up menu and explore the Plug-In Store. After selecting a plug-in, confirm installation, and enable the plug-in to begin using it. You can only install up to three plug-ins at a time. As with all applications, you'll also want to verify the function of the plug-in and its creator, and consider if it is safe and ethical to use before installing.

Plug-ins installed on ChatGPT function the same way the basic platform does, requiring users to input prompts in order to "chat" with the application. The application will attempt to provide you with the data you need based on your plug-ins. ChatGPT also includes the option to target a plug-in by including it in the prompt. If your results don't appear to be specific enough, you can ask the program to complete a task and direct it to a particular plug-in by name—for example, "Help me find a review on this book using A Review Summary."

Now that you understand how to install and activate plug-ins, we'll cover a few that authors might find useful.

TIMEPORT

Perfect for the average Speculative Fiction writer, with Timeport, ChatGPT can become a speculative time travel game, imagining scenes, environments, scenarios, people, and things from somewhere in the future. Timeport can spit out details that are excellent for shaking loose the mentally stuck writer's creative reserves. An article by *PCMag* about Timeport identifies text outputs after a user prompted, "I want to travel to the year 5000." The result was a paragraph of ample description that included hovering vehicles, holographic communicators, and nano-technology—all things befitting a story set in the future. Timeport may not be the best plug-in if you want cold-hard facts, but if you're a Sci-Fi author desperate to dislodge an underperforming imagination, Timeport might be worth exploring.

Pro Tip: If you ever get stuck, remember Timeport is an add-on to ChatGPT and can receive prompts just like the base AI program. When in doubt, simply ask the chatbot, "What do I do next?"

AI QUEST

Similar to Timeport, AI Quest produces a text-based adventure based on your prompts. Are you looking for a Romantic Comedy in the style of Tim Burton? AI Quest will ask you for a name and age range, then subject and style. It will follow up with text descriptions of the scenario and a set of choices you can make. Once you've decided the path you'd like to explore, you can enter it and let ChatGPT guide you.

While Timeport aims to deliver ideas about a specific time period, AI Quest will output a literal quest laden with details for you to use. If you have a story that's partially written or outlined but you're stuck on where to go next, AI Quest could help you explore the next steps your characters could take.

If you're concerned about your intellectual property becoming part of the overall language model, consider removing specific details about your story from your prompt, such as names, places, and unique ideas. Keeping it bare-bones may still be enough for the program's results to spark inspiration.

Pro Tip: AI Quest is a facet of ChatGPT, meaning it can remember your historical queries within ChatGPT. Want to try a different set of outcomes but don't want to re-type your previous prompts? Ask ChatGPT to "remember" your last output—then ask it for another variation using that output.

A REVIEW SUMMARY

As authors, we are accustomed to looking at reviews, but analyzing a large collection of them can be time-consuming. If you wanted only a summarized version of the best and worst reviews on a specific Amazon listing or need a breakdown of what readers are saying about your books from a sky-level view, A Review Summary might be the answer.

To use the plug-in, simply ask for "a summary review" of a product on Amazon using a prompt in ChatGPT, and the plug-in will import and summarize a few notable reviews that contain a rating.

Beyond studying their own books, authors might find value in importing multiple prompts for reviews of similarly written books—such as books in the also-bought section or those by comparative authors—and asking ChatGPT to point out what readers are saying similarly across them. The results may highlight tropes or frequently noted keywords readers input in their reviews.

Pro Tip: In the end, we must be responsible for our own research, and relying on ChatGPT's outputs to be accurate one hundred percent of the time is not a good move. Always double-check your findings. ChatGPT can save us time, but it cannot replace an author with a strong attention to detail.

A NOTE ON AI ETHICS

With any AI-generated output, be sure to double-check your work, fact-check when needed, and otherwise ensure your writing is of the caliber you desire. Take care you are using programs ethically and legally—don't upload other creatives' work into a platform without permission, and keep up-to-date on discussions about the use of AI. Know that the conversations around AI are constantly shifting and adapting as the programs continue to evolve.

Plug-ins are the bits at the end of your drill chuck; the right bit fits the right screw. There is an amalgamation of plug-ins being developed on the regular, and jumping into modifying an already intense application like ChatGPT can be daunting. However, by keeping focused on what you need and experimenting with the options available, you can determine which plug-ins best suit your needs and find a combination that works for your author business. ■

David Viergutz

David Viergutz

David Viergutz is a disabled Army Veteran, Law Enforcement Veteran, husband and proud father. He is an author of stories from every flavor of horror and dark fiction. One day, David's wife sat him down and gave him the confidence to start putting his imagination on paper. From then on out his creativity has no longer been stifled by self-doubt and he continues to write with a smile on his face in a dark, candle-lit room.

Not Your Grandma's Grim-Dark

COZY FANTASY'S OTHERWORLDLY SETTINGS, LIGHTHEARTED ESCAPISM OFFER READERS WHAT THEY'VE BEEN CRAVING

In February 2022, when Travis Baldree self-published his smashingly successful book *Legends and Lattes,* legions of readers found themselves craving more of a genre they likely weren't even aware existed. It's called Cozy Fantasy, and some of its most common tropes have been around for decades, even if the genre label hasn't.

From the opening of *The Hobbit* to *Redwall* and *The Princess Bride*, readers' favorite Fantasy books have often included scenes that leave them feeling warm, fuzzy, and longing for more time with their characters and their world. The unsettled nature of the last few years has left some readers searching for books with less darkness and less danger around every corner, and Cozy Fantasy sales have skyrocketed as a result.

So what exactly is Cozy Fantasy? This subgenre of Fantasy marries fan-favorite tropes like epic quests, action-packed fight scenes, and mythical creatures with the common emotional elements and settings found in traditional Cozy tales. The key to this genre's success is creating characters and fully immersive worlds that evoke a feeling of comfort, family, and overall lightheartedness.

Unlike traditional Fantasy, where the fate of the world hangs in the balance, the stakes in Cozy Fantasy don't have to be quite so high. Readers are just as drawn to stories with lower stakes and high emotional value. Good still triumphs over evil, and ordinary everyday characters still become heroes, but it all happens on a smaller scale. It's been said of the genre that it's less about saving the world and more about saving the neighborhood. Like many Cozy genre fans, readers also seem to prefer less violence, gore, and despicable bad guys than those typically found in Epic Fantasy.

Alongside the recent explosive popularity of the genre, several resources for authors wanting to try their hand at writing a Cozy Fantasy have emerged. While the following list is far from all-inclusive, it serves as a great starting point for dipping your quill in the inkwell of this lucrative genre.

RESOURCES

Wyngraf Magazine
Website: https://wyngraf.com

According to the magazine's website, "Wyngraf was founded to promote and encourage fantasy stories that focus on the little things: friends, family, home, travel. Our authors create worlds that readers get lost in… and dream of someday visiting." The site contains articles, flash fiction, and submission guidelines for authors wanting to pitch stories for the publication's open submission calls.

r/CozyFantasy
Website: https://reddit.com/r/CozyFantasy

The subreddit with 3500 members discusses all things Cozy Fantasy and can offer a diverse and comprehensive overview of what readers like. It's also a great place to meet potential readers.

Goodreads—Cozy Fantasy Books list
Website: https://goodreads.com/shelf/show/cozy-fantasy

This list of over two thousand titles that readers have shelved as Cozy Fantasy is an excellent resource for authors looking to read and research popular titles within the genre. Reader ratings and comments provide insight into reader expectations of the genre.

Cozy Vales
Website: https://cozyvales.com
Facebook: https://facebook.com/cozyvales

This is a new Cozy Fantasy shared world featuring work by multiple indie authors from a variety of genres. Their Facebook reader group details how the authors created and structured the world and offers a place to connect with other Cozy Fantasy authors and readers. The group's website is still a work-in-progress, but it contains a sign-up link to their Golden Acorn newsletter, which adds a fun and creative element to the world-building aspect of Cozy Vales.

As a genre, Cozy Fantasy seems to have found a niche filled with readers hungry for more. Audiences don't seem to be concerned whether an author is traditionally or self-published; as long as you can craft a story and characters that leave them feeling content that all's right with the world, you'll have faithful fans who will be eager to revisit your world as soon as the next title drops. ■

Jenn Mitchell

Jenn Mitchell

Jenn Mitchell writes Urban Fantasy and Weird West, as well as culinary cozy mysteries under the pen name, J Lee Mitchell. She writes, cooks, and gardens in the heart of South Central Pennsylvania's Amish Country. When she's not doing these things, she dreams of training llama riding ninjas.

She enjoys traveling, quilting, hoarding cookbooks, Sanntangling, and spending time with the World's most patient and loving significant other.

Taking Care of Business

This month's topic might be my favorite of the entire year: the business of writing. Why? Because I've long said, as writers, we must treat what we do as a business.

That doesn't just mean building a writing routine or dedicating time to marketing your work in between releases. Those are great things to do, don't get me wrong, but treating your author career like a business means looking at the financial side of things too—the true "business" part of the equation.

It means you behave accordingly while managing your business by forming an entity, an employer identification number, and a business bank account, as well as setting up the right support so you can operate like a business owner.

Creatives can sometimes drag their feet when tackling finances and other administrative work, but this month I want to help you shift your perception and your procedure to give your author career room to grow. And I've got another four hundred words to help you get there, so let's dive into it.

PERCEPTION

The perception that business people can't be artists and vice versa is, to be direct, wrong. Here's the thing: you might have been told that to be creative is to court the muse. "You must write only when you're struck with magnificent inspiration," you might've heard. There may have been mention of the dangers of writer's block for good measure.

In addition, there's the prevailing belief that we're either right-brained or left-brained. Honestly, I don't know which one is supposed to be inclined to be creative or business, and it doesn't matter.

The truth is, you've got both sides available to you at all times. Now it's true that you might have sharpened your creativity tools while neglecting your business muscles over the years. Just like getting in shape, the muscles we focus on grow, and the muscles we neglect atrophy.

If you're a brilliant creative, chances are this is the side of you that is the strongest and receives the most attention. As an author, your writing, design, and marketing tasks can keep those muscles strong, so you can spare some time to shore up the ones that need attention. Which brings us to…

PROCEDURE

I'll be honest with you. This part—learning things you don't know and getting better in areas where you're weak—can be frustrating and confusing. I know, I'm a ray of sunshine, right? But you want to make a prosperous living as a writer, so you're going to have to shine a light in those dark places. Not to worry, I've intentionally made it sound more ominous than necessary, so what I propose now won't seem so terrible.

Before you were a boss at writing, you studied the craft, your genre, and read a lot of other books to build your writing skills. How you proceed about the business side of writing is the same, except this time, you can create a shortcut. Instead of doing the studying yourself, engage the services of professionals to help.

It's true you'll want to know a few things, like what EBITDA stands for—earnings before interest, taxes, depreciation, and amortization—or how to draft agreements and contracts for anyone you hire as part of your business. But you don't need to know everything; you just need to know the right people. Have someone on call who can help you make big decisions. Having a mentor, someone who has real-world experience and results, is also great. Your bookkeeper and CPA can help guide your ship when it comes to tracking earnings and expenses via spreadsheet, and they'll be worth their weight in gold. As you grow your business over time, you'll build the connections you need to keep growing.

WHY IT'S IMPORTANT

I would be remiss if I didn't share why understanding business and how to run your writing career like one is beneficial, so if you'll indulge me a couple hundred more words, I'll do just that.

You'll attract more business. You'll carry yourself with confidence, and confidence is magnetic.

You'll write more, more efficiently, and more effectively. A business person understands they have to generate product to generate revenue. Once you understand the connection, you'll write like it's your job—because it is.

You'll make more money. I saved the best for last! Run your business like a business, and your business will pay you like one.

One more important thought before I go: you can do this. You can learn about business and turn your writing into a solid, prosperous, productive career.

Happy writing! ∎

Honorée Corder

Honorée Corder

Honorée Corder is the author of more than fifty books, an empire builder, and encourager of writers. When she's not writing, she's spoiling her dog and two cats, eating something fabulous her husband made on the grill, working out, or reading. She hopes this article made a positive impact on your life, and if it did, you'll reach out to her via HonoreeCorder.com.

Getting Things Done with GTD

The year may be winding down, but plenty of authors likely still have a lot of tasks on their indie author to-do list—and that's in addition to holiday shopping. The more information in your head, the harder it is to know where to focus. Add enough to your plate, and you may just end up thinking about what you should be doing or worrying you'll forget something rather than focusing on what you're actually doing.

The Getting Things Done (GTD) personal productivity method, created by David Allen in 2001, may be the key to helping you better manage your time.

CLEAR THE CHAOS

GTD works by helping you visualize what needs doing by organizing tasks into five bite-sized actions that make completion easier. You're not limited to any specific collection tool to clear your mental clutter, so choose one you'll use. Your collection tool could be a notebook, a to-do list app, or a web-based productivity tool. Just be sure it's versatile enough to handle complex projects.

From there, use the following five steps to help define your tasks and determine actionable steps to organize the chaos of your mental to-do list:

Capture anything that needs action, and list the item in your collection tool.

Clarify if each item is actionable, reference material, a future task, or trash. Consider whether you can do the task in less than two minutes or if it's a project with multiple steps. You may also have reference materials—an article or email you can file until you're ready to act. Identify the desired outcome, and determine tasks you're ready to take action on now. If you lack time or energy, or a task doesn't advance you toward your current goal, move it to future tasks.

Organize tasks by breaking them down into the smallest actionable components. Add a reminder for a task to your calendar, delegate it, file it as reference materials, or park the task for future action.

Reflect on and review your system at a scheduled date and time. This could mean completing a quick daily review in the morning to stay on track with a once-a-week in-depth review of your list. Frequent reviews ensure you aren't just doing things but doing the right things at the right time.

Engage and get to work. Using your system helps you know what to work on and when by knowing the action, its priority, your available time, and your energy levels.

Depending on your task list, GTD may seem tedious at first, but the time and energy invested in setting up the system can pay off with consistent use. Even if you only apply some steps of GTD, picking up a habit or two can help you be less stressed and more productive, which will reduce the mental strain on your brain. ■

Maureen Bonatch

Maureen Bonatch

"Maureen Bonatch MSN, RN, is a fiction author and freelance healthcare writer. Her experience as a fiction author helps her create engaging and creative content as she authors numerous healthcare articles and online educational content. Maureen writes cozy paranormal mysteries as M.L. Bonatch and urban fantasy, paranormal romance, and other genres as Maureen Bonatch.

When Maureen's not doing the bidding of a feisty Shih Tzu, she's a mom to twin daughters, exploring the beautiful woods of PA with her hubby and dancing as much as possible. She believes in pairing music with every mood, that laughter is contagious, and caffeine and wine are essential for survival. She is the owner of MaureenBonatch.com and CharmedType.com. "

An Easier Way for Authors to Boost Sales with BookBub

Plenty of indie authors tout the magic of BookBub for its Featured Deal promotions. These elusive deals can help spike sales, of course, but they're not the only way BookBub can help you find new readers.

When it comes to advertising, you may think BookBub ads are only for books that are free or $0.99. But that is not how I use them.

On Facebook, authors who want to target the fans of certain authors with their ads can only do so for a handful of big names, such as Lee Child or Terry Pratchett. However, on BookBub, you can target almost anyone making worthwhile sales.

Let's say, for example, that you write a Cozy Mystery with a dog in it and want to target me because your covers and stories are similar in flavor to mine.

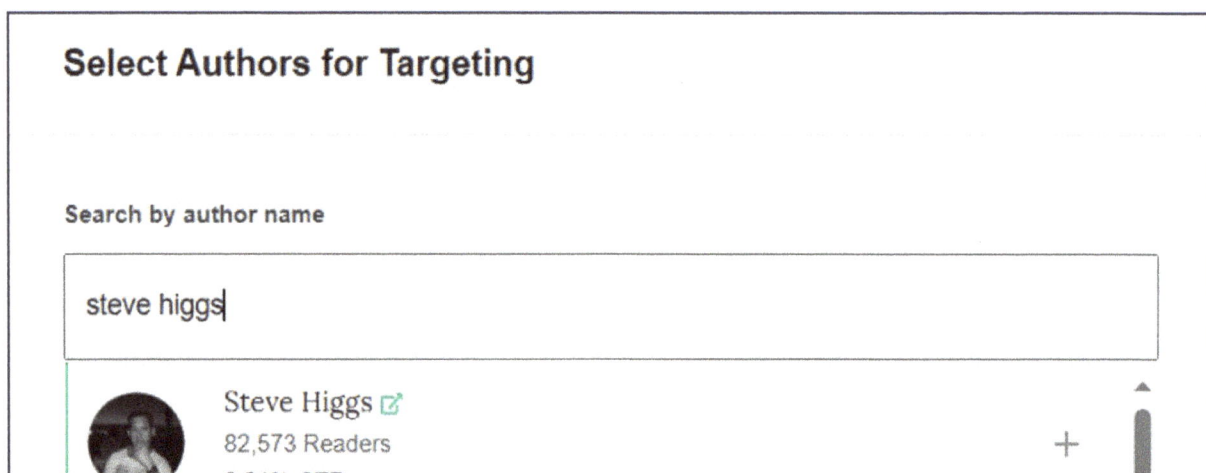

The author targeting section on BookBub Ads

By targeting me—or, more accurately, my readers—with your ads, you can aim your ad directly at the readers who like my books. In some cases, the pool of potential readers you're targeting will be small compared with the audiences you can find on Facebook. However, these are readers whose interest in books is sufficient to make them subscribe to a daily email.

You can test out comparable authors for just a few bucks and find out if their readers will be attracted to your books.

WHY IT WORKS

I don't have the column space to explain all the reasons you want to target successful authors with BookBub ads, so here is the biggest one: Amazon ads are all about relevance. New books have no sales data, so those titles have no relevance. But you know what books and authors should be good targets for your ads, and you can game the system by using BookBub to connect your books to those with sales data.

This is how it works:

Target the author of your choice with BookBub ads.

Sell enough books to show up in that author's also-bought section, meaning you're now relevant and have sales data on Amazon.

Push more traffic to that author with Amazon ads.

AD CREATION

For my BookBub ads, I use the same images and captions as I do for Facebook ads. The pixel width and height are different, but most image platforms, such as Book Brush, have automated templates to account for this.

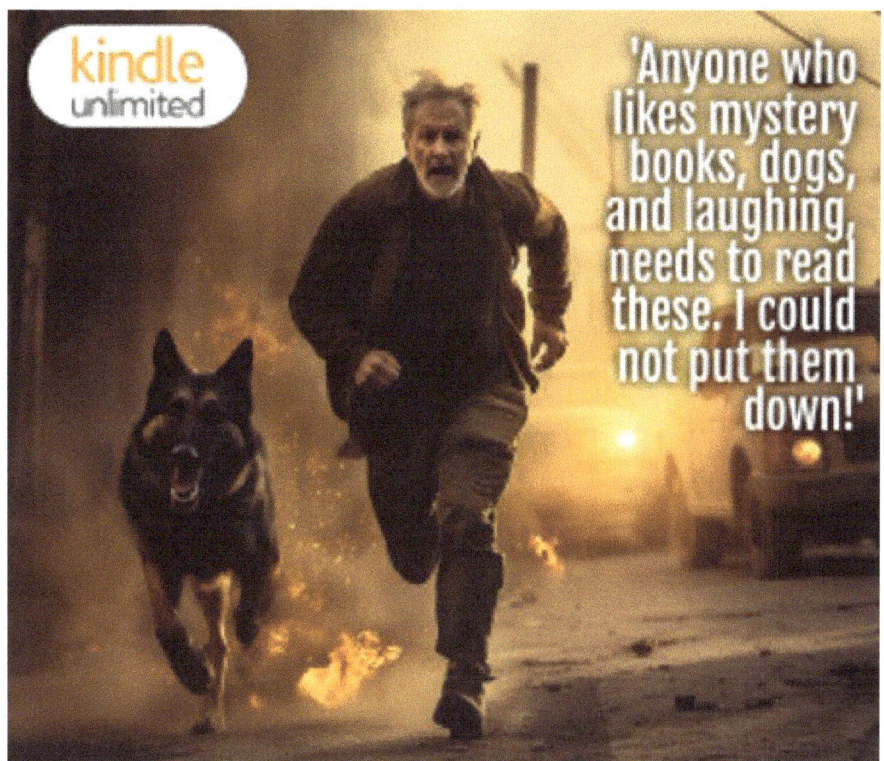

The image from a recent ad I ran

One good thing about BookBub is that you only need to worry about the image. There is no space for clever copy or headlines, so use images that worked for your Facebook ads and just give them a great caption.

SETTING UP YOUR CAMPAIGN

In my BookBub ad campaigns, I use cost-per-click (CPC) instead of cost-per-thousand (CPM). Many may argue with this, but if your ads get no clicks, it costs you nothing using CPC. BookBub will suggest a bid range, and I usually go a few cents over the minimum and run ads continuously at a low budget of $5 per day. I then shut them off if they don't sell books.

How do I know if they are selling? I use Amazon Attribution Links to track individual sales for each ad I run. You can remove the guesswork and gain data to analyze by giving each ad a unique link.

Sep 29	Oct 01	Oct 03	Oct 05	Oct 07	Oct 09	Oct 11	Oct 13	Oct 15	Oct 17	Oct 19	Oct 21	Oct 23	Oct 25	Oct 27	Oct 29

New ad group | Search by ad group name | Columns ˅ Time unit: Daily ˅ Date range: Sep 30 – Oct 30, 2023 ˅ | Export

Ad group ⓘ	Channel ⓘ	Publisher ⓘ	Click-throughs ⓘ	DPV ⓘ	Purchases ⓘ ˅	Units sold ⓘ	KENP read ⓘ	[MS]	Estimated KENP
Rex 10 ad 13 588104800791268110	Social	Facebook	16,713	17,060	97	97	88,337		
Rex 10 ad 2 592107764204283889	Social	Facebook	4,896	5,027	40	40	17,967		
Rex 10 ad 3 590532630992472875	Social	Facebook	1,408	1,493	11	11	12,982		
Rex 10 BB ad 1 594303372415991722	Social	Bookbub	593	643	10	10	8,633		
Rex 10 ad 5 581016537668467199	Social	Facebook	1,095	1,039	8	8	5,976		

The campaign for one of my boxed sets. Fourth from the top is an ad group with BookBub in the title.

When you are setting up the attribution links, just click "New" in the Select A Publisher section and type in "BookBub." In the ad group name, create a designation that makes it clear this ad is on BookBub. When you revisit to monitor your results, you will be able to see at a glance if the ad is generating sales.

Add ad groups and specify platforms and channels where your campaign is running on.

Ad group 1

Ad group name

Publisher ⓘ

Channel ⓘ

Select a publisher
Select a publisher
New
About
AdRoll
ADTV
Aki Technologies
Amnet

Enter a name for the unique attribution tag you are creating.

Choose the website, app, or other property where your media will be displayed.

The ad type (for example Display, Video, Social, Search, or Email).

Click "New" in the Select A Publisher section and type in" BookBub" to help accurately track your ads' performance on the platform using Amazon Attribution.

BookBub's Featured Deals earn plenty of attention among indie authors, but don't overlook your advertising opportunities with the platform. Get the image and audience right, and you should see very good sales. ▪

Steve Higgs

Steve Higgs

High school Valedictorian enlists in the Marine Corps under a guaranteed tank contract. An inauspicious start that was quickly superseded by excelling in language study.

YOUR ONE-STOP RESOURCE

INDIE AUTHOR TOOLS

INDIEAUTHORTOOLS.COM

📚 Over 45+ categories of resources, from AI to website builders, all designed to supercharge your self-publishing journey.

✍️ Authentic reviews and real-world case studies from authors who've used these tools to bring their creative visions to life.

👤 A community-powered project, crowdsourced by authors who know exactly what you need because they've been there too!

🚀 Boost your authorial prowess with our popular weekly newsletter, packed with tips, tricks, and updates on the latest tools.

www.ingramcontent.com/pod-product-compliance
Lightning Source LLC
Chambersburg PA
CBHW052345210326
41597CB00037B/6262